Home Office Research Study 150

Predicting reoffending for Discretionary Conditional Release

by
John B Copas, Peter Marshall and Roger Tarling

A Research and Statistics Directorate Report

Home Office
Research and
Statistics
Directorate

London: Home Office

Home Office Research Studies

The Home Office Research Studies are reports on research undertaken by or on behalf of the Home Office. They cover the range of subjects for which the Home Secretary has responsibility. Titles in the series are listed at the back of this report (copies are available from the address on the back cover). Other publications produced by the Research and Statistics Directorate include Research Findings, the Research Bulletin, Statistical Bulletins and Statistical Paper.

The Research and Statistics Directorate

The Directorate consists of three Units which deal with research and statistics on Crime and Criminal Justice, Offenders and Corrections, Immigration and General matters; the Programme Development Unit; the Economics Unit; and the Operational Research Unit.

 The Research and Statistics Directorate is an integral part of the Home Office, serving the Ministers and the department itself, its services, Parliament and the public through research, development and statistics. Information and knowledge from these sources informs policy development and the management of programmes; their dissemination improves wider public understanding of matters of Home Office concern.

First published 1996

Application for reproduction should be made to the Information Section, Home Office, Room 278, 50 Queen Anne's Gate, London SW1H 9AT.

©Crown copyright 1996 ISBN 1 85893 5768
ISSN 0072-6435

Foreword

It is important when making decisions to draw on past experience. Statistical risk predictors for parole do this by examining and summarising the offending history of a large number of prisoners. This knowledge can be used in guiding decisions to release future prisoners with similar characteristics. Risk predictors should be constructed using the most relevant data and the best available methods. It is also important to publish the technical details of the work so that they may be publicly scrutinised and available to inform subsequent developmental work. This report describes the Risk of Reconviction (ROR) score which has been developed to assist the Parole Board adjudicate in its decisions whether to grant discretionary conditional release.

CHRISTOPHER NUTTALL
Director of Research and Statistics

Acknowledgements

Many people helped in the course of the project: Terry Russell and staff of the Parole Board, Secretariat located files and coded much of the data. Colleagues in RSD, Diane Caddle, John Ditchfield, Richard Harries and Mike Lock, assisted with data collection, providing background statistics and with drawing a suitable sample from administrative records. Tony Fowles and Rita Maurice, two members of the Parole Board, gave invaluable practical advice in the latter stages of the project, in particular on how the results of our work should be implemented by the Parole Board. We would like to record our thanks to each and every one of them.

JOHN B COPAS

PETER MARSHALL

ROGER TARLING

Contents

Summary

Statistical risk prediction has been a feature of parole decision making since the inception of parole in the 1960s. Until recently the Reconviction Prediction Score (RPS), which estimated the likelihood that an offender would be reconvicted within two years following release from prison, has been used in parole decision making.

In the mid 1980s, however, the Carlisle Committee was set up to review the system of early release of prisoners. The Committee recommended radical changes which were eventually enacted in the 1991 Criminal Justice Act. Parole was replaced by discretionary conditional release (still commonly called parole) but unlike the previous parole it was restricted to offenders serving four years or over.

The Carlisle Committee, and subsequent directives from the Home Secretary, emphasised the need for the Parole Board to take into account the likelihood that a prisoner would reoffend, particularly the risk that he would commit a serious offence, during the period of DCR. As the RPS was not suitable for use under the new arrangements, a new statistical risk predictor, the Risk of Reconviction (ROR), was developed.

The ROR was constructed by examining many background characteristics of over 1,200 offenders discharged from prison in 1987. Also gathered was information on offenders' criminal careers for the period after 1987. The statistical analysis identified six characteristics which were important and could be used to estimate the likelihood of reoffending. The six characteristics were: age at conviction, number of youth custody sentences, number of adult custodial sentences, number of previous convictions, type of offence committed and sex of the offender. Information on these six characteristics are incorporated into the ROR. In fact the information is used to construct two risk scores; one for serious reoffending and one for any reoffending (although minor summary offences, in particular, minor motoring offences are omitted from the definition of "any offence"). The two scores can be used to estimate the probability that an offender will reoffend in a given period. These estimates form part of a set of information available to the Parole Board when adjudicating individual cases.

1 Introduction

The Carlisle Committee was set up in the mid 1980s to review the system of early release of prisoners. The Committee reported in 1988 and its recommendations were incorporated into the 1990 White Paper *Crime, Justice and Protecting the Public*. These recommendations were enacted in the 1991 Criminal Justice Act and eventually came into operation in October 1992.

New arrangements for early release

In brief, the new arrangements abolished parole for people serving sentences of less than four years in prison. Instead, offenders awarded such sentences after 1 October 1992 are automatically released at the halfway point of their sentence (unless days are added on to the sentence as a punishment for disciplinary offences in prison). After this point the person is supervised in the community until the three-quarters point of their sentence, or until the 100 per cent point if they were convicted of a sexual offence and this extended supervision was ordered by the court. As these prisoners are released automatically, the Parole Board plays no part in determining when they are released from prison, hence this group is not considered further in this report.

Under the new arrangements, prisoners serving four years or over are considered for discretionary conditional release (DCR)[1] in much the same way as before, but with the decision being wholly taken by the Parole Board (although the Home Secretary's ability to veto a decision remains unaltered).[2] However, rather than being eligible at the one-third point as previously, these prisoners are eligible for DCR at the halfway point of their sentence. If not released at the halfway point or before the two-thirds point, they are automatically released at the two-thirds point (unless any days have been added on for disciplinary offences). Whether released early or automatically at the two-thirds point, prisoners are supervised in the community by a probation officer until the three-quarters point of their sentence (which can be extended for sexual offenders in the same way as for short sentence prisoners).

---

1   The term Discretionary Conditional Release (DCR) has yet to be wholeheartedly adopted, and early release is still commonly called parole. The terms will be used interchangeably throughout the report.

2   Under the pre-1992 system of parole Local Review Committees (LRCs) took the initial decision whether or not to recommend a prisoner to the Parole Board for consideration.

An important element of the CJA 1991 was thus the introduction of a period of mandatory supervision in the community for all prisoners – at least from the two-thirds point to the three-quarters point of a sentence if unsuccessful when considered for DCR, longer if successful. The Parole Board has discretion to release a prisoner into the community anywhere between the halfway point and the two-thirds point of a sentence. For a prisoner sentenced to four years in custody this "parole window" is eight months, but longer for prisoners given longer sentences.

The need for a risk predictor

The Carlisle Committee and the Home Secretary (in his directions to the Parole Board, issued at the time the new arrangements came into effect) both expressed particular concern about the possibility of a parolee offending when he might otherwise have been in prison, that is, during the "parole window".

> *"The parole decision will, thus, be based upon an evaluation of the risk to the public of the person committing a further serious offence at a time when he would otherwise be in prison...."* (Carlisle Committee Report p79)

To assist the Parole Board in coming to a decision in individual cases the Carlisle Committee recommended that in considering a prisoner for release on parole, the Board should take account of the best statistical indicators of risk available at that time:

> *"We believe that the Board should be under a duty to take into account statistical prediction techniques and, where appropriate, clinical assessments which will assist it in its work."* (Carlisle Committee Report, p81)

The requirement to consider estimates of the risk of reoffending are also included in the Home Secretary's directions – see Report of the Parole Board for 1993, Appendix A.

Statistical prediction instruments have been developed to aid decision making in criminal justice, especially decisions to grant parole (Farrington and Tarling, 1985). Indeed such a predictor, the Reconviction Prediction Score (RPS), has been in use since the inception of parole in the 1960s (Nuttall *et al*, 1977). The RPS was revalidated and modified in the 1980s (Ward 1987) and predicts the likelihood that a prisoner will be convicted of a new offence within two years of release from prison.

The recommendations of the Carlisle Committee, and the subsequent 1991 Criminal Justice Act, heralded a number of changes (as noted above) which suggested that the RPS would not be suitable for use after implementation of the Act. First, following the Act, discretionary release was restricted to people serving determinate custodial sentences of four years or more whereas the RPS was developed for use with parole-eligible prisoners (apart from female and juvenile prisoners and lifers), most of whom were serving sentences of less than four years. Thus the intended target population was substantially different after implementation of the CJA 1991.

Second, the Carlisle Committee expressed concern about the risk of a parolee committing a new offence when he or she would otherwise have been in custody (as the offence could have been avoided had the offender remained in prison). The RPS could not assess this risk as it estimates the likelihood of reconviction within two years of release. There is often a substantial delay between a person committing an offence and being caught by the police, and then again between arrest and conviction. (For the sample of prisoners included in this study there was an average delay of six months between the commission of an offence and conviction of it.)

A third shortcoming of the RPS was that it only estimated risk for a fixed two-year period after release. Under the new arrangements the Parole Board was to give consideration to the likelihood that an offender would commit an offence during the time he or she could be on parole. This period (the "parole window") would vary between offenders depending on the sentence they had been given and it could also change over time for the same offender if he or she was denied parole at the first opportunity. Thus, for the Parole Board to take account of an offender's likelihood of committing further offences it needed an estimate of risk that changed as the "parole window" changed.

A further recommendation of the Carlisle Committee, which became part of the Home Secretary's directions to the Parole Board, was that more weight should be given to the risk, albeit smaller, of a potential parolee committing a serious offence than the greater risk of him or her committing a less serious offence while on parole. The RPS is unable to make a distinction between the relative risks of different kinds of offences.

For the above reasons, and the added consideration that RPS was developed using data on prisoners released in the late 1960s (though revalidated using data on prisoners released in the years 1977 to 1979), it was felt that a new predictor was needed. Furthermore, it was agreed that the new predictor should fulfil the following requirements: it should be up to date; it should give an estimate of the likelihood of a potential parolee committing a new offence (of which he was eventually convicted) within a range of periods after his or her release from prison; and it should include a separate estimate of the likelihood of committing a serious offence.

The purpose of this report is to describe the development of the Risk of Reconviction (ROR) to be used by the Parole Board as an aid to decision making.

The design of the study, a brief description of the sample and the data collected are described in the following chapter. Details of the statistical analysis used to construct the ROR are set out in Chapter 3. This chapter need not be read by those not concerned with the technical underpinnings of the ROR. The ROR is described in simple terms in Chapter 4 along with its practical application.

2 Design of the study

The design of the study raised several conceptual and methodological issues which needed to be addressed before data could be collected.

It was stated in the previous chapter that the Parole Board is instructed to pay particular attention to the prisoner's likelihood of committing a serious offence while on parole as well as taking into account the prisoner's likelihood of committing any offence during this period. It was decided, therefore, to develop two prediction instruments; the first to predict 'any' reoffence, the second to predict a 'serious' reoffence. 'Any' reoffence and 'serious' reoffence had to be operationally defined. 'Any' posed few problems and includes any offence that is recorded in an offender's criminal record (violence, sexual or property offences). It should be emphasised, however, that it excludes most summary offences, in the main the vast majority of minor motoring offences.

Despite common usage there is no agreed definition of a 'serious' offence and the research literature shows that no two people always agree on what constitutes a serious offence (Pease 1988). The Carlisle Committee did not offer any definition. Seriousness cannot simply be equated with the type of offence, for example, not all violent offences are serious and not all serious offences are violent. Some sexual offences are committed by people who freely consent. After much discussion the difficulty was circumvented by relying on sentencers' assessment of the new offence – thus a serious reoffence was defined as one which resulted in the imposition of a new custodial sentence.

Parolees can be returned to prison for reasons other than committing a new offence. However, for both any reoffence and serious reoffence it was decided from the outset not to include revocation of a parole licence unless it was accompanied by conviction for a new offence.

The requirement to predict when reoffences occur during a period of time, where the period varies between offenders, posed several methodological problems. What was needed was information on whether a prisoner reoffended following release from prison and, if he or she did, the exact date the offence was committed. As with all other studies of this kind no information is available on offences offenders commit but for which they are not caught.

Reoffending had therefore to be confined to offences which subsequently resulted in conviction. The dates of offences committed within two years were obtained by first noting whether the offender had been convicted of a further offence at any time during the four years following his release from prison. Information on convictions is readily available from the Offenders Index (a computerised database maintained by the Home Office) and from the Police National Identification Service (NIS). If convictions were recorded against the offender the date the offence was committed was extracted from the NIS.

The sample

The prediction instrument needed to be available shortly after implementation of the new arrangements for conditional release which came into effect in October 1992. This imposed a restriction on the design of the study which had to be carried out retrospectively, detailed information could not be gathered from interviews with prisoners, nor from records on current prisoners. Furthermore, as four years had to have elapsed the sample was drawn from offenders discharged from prison in 1987.

A rough power calculation for the research suggested that a minimum sample of about 1,000 would be needed. In order to ensure a final sample of this size or greater, 60 per cent of the male prisoners discharged in 1987 who had been serving sentences of four years or more were selected at random. This resulted in an initial sample of 1,590 men.

It was accepted from the start that, given the numbers of cases required for the research, and the few women sentenced to, and discharged from, prison following sentences of four years or more, to develop a separate predictor for women was not practicable. Instead all women discharged in 1986 and 1987 from sentences of four years or more were selected; a total of 78 women.

The cases needed to be matched on several different databases and substantial numbers were expected not to be matched successfully, thus resulting in some attrition of the initial sample. Cases were lost at the following points:

• manual tracing of parole numbers (needed to trace parole dossiers)

• manual tracing of parole dossiers

• computerised tracing of criminal history at Offenders Index.

About 20 per cent of men and a quarter of the women could not be traced, resulting in a final sample of 1,191 men and 56 women.

The data

Information was collated from the Prison Index, parole dossiers, Offenders Index and NIS files on many characteristics for each member of the sample. Choice of information was guided by previous prediction studies – all characteristics used in the development of the Reconviction Prediction Score were included in the study – and by the type of information routinely available in the source documents. Compromises had to be made in defining some variables in order to conform with statistical packages.

From the Offenders Index information was obtained on whether or not a person had been reconvicted after release from prison in 1987, and if he or she had, whether or not this conviction had resulted in a new prison sentence.

For those ex-prisoners with new convictions the date of the commission of the offence was traced at National Identification Service (NIS) in New Scotland Yard. In cases in which the actual date of commission was not available, the date of arrest was used in the analysis. In the absence of date of arrest the date of conviction was used. This may have resulted in a slight bias causing some offences appearing to have been committed later than they actually were, but this effect was unavoidable and occurred in very few cases.

The variables coded and available for analysis are listed below.

Demographic and socio-economic variables

- Sex
- Age at conviction
- Ethnic group
- Social class
- Number of years spent in full-time education
- Employment status at time of offence
- Employment plans on release from prison
- Time in last job
- Living arrangements at time of offence i.e. alone, with parents, with spouse
- Living arrangements on release from prison
- Marital status at time of release from prison
- Particular problems, i.e. gambling, drugs, alcohol.

Criminal history variables

- Length of current prison sentence
- Type of offence
- Number of associates
- Age at first conviction
- Number of previous convictions
- Number of previous convictions for property offences
- Number of previous convictions for violent offences
- Number of previous convictions for sexual offences
- Number of youth custody sentences
- Number of adult custodial sentences
- Number of supervision orders
- Number of probation orders
- Number of prison disciplinary offences while in prison
- Type of prison disciplinary offences.

Reoffending follow-up variables

- Whether reconvicted following release from prison
- Dates of subsequent reconvictions
- Dates offences (which resulted in reconviction) were committed
- Time between release from prison and first reoffence
- Type of offences committed
- Sentences awarded at reconviction.

3. Development of the Risk of Reconviction (ROR) score

This chapter describes the statistical analysis used to develop the new Risk of Reconviction (ROR) score. The main sections cover the preliminary analysis of the data, the details of the statistical technique adopted for the ROR score, and the details of the ROR itself. Two versions of the ROR were developed, one for all reoffending (any reoffences leading to a conviction) and another for serious reoffending (any reoffences leading to a further prison sentence).

The methodology used in developing the original Reconviction Prediction Score, RPS, was essentially to select those factors which appeared significantly associated with reconviction, and then to form a weighted sum of the selected factors with weights reflecting the degree of association between each factor and the presence or absence of a reconviction within two years. The RPS estimates the risk of reconviction within a fixed period of time after release. The new procedures, however, required the assessment of the risk of reoffending within a variable time period, as the period of potential parole varies from one prisoner to the next. For this a more flexible approach was needed.

The development of the ROR was based on statistical modelling, the basic idea being to formulate an accurate mathematical description of the way in which each factor influences reoffending. The modelling approach has some important advantages over the methodology used for the RPS. First, the resulting score is usually simpler in that it is based on fewer factors. Second, it takes proper account of the intercorrelations between the different factors and allows for the possibility that the effect of one factor may be masked by that of another. Third, a statistical model produces a concise description of what has been observed in the data and has a clear scientific rationale capable of independent verification.

Finding the probability of a reoffence occurring over different time periods is equivalent to finding the probability distribution of the time to the first such reoffence. This is somewhat analogous to survival analysis used by actuaries in assessing the distribution of the time to death, or length of survival, of purchasers of life insurance policies. Their methods are now widely used by medical statisticians and reliability engineers, and can be adapted for use in the analysis of recidivism data, as shown in Schmidt and Witte (1988) and Tarling (1993).

Preliminary analysis

A large number of factors were measured for the prisoners in the sample. Factors were examined one at a time in order to assess their association with reoffending and hence their potential influence for prediction. This was done by taking a fixed time period, here taken as two years to be consistent with the RPS, and tabulating the percentage reoffending within two years against values of each of these factors. For factors taking a large number of values, such as age at conviction or number of previous convictions, a graph of percentage reoffending within ranges of factor values was plotted. Figure 3.1, for example, shows the data for number of previous convictions. Here the sample is divided into ten equally sized groups using adjacent ranges, and the points show the percentage reoffending plotted against the average number of previous convictions within each group.

Figure 3.1
Reoffending (2 years) against Number of Previous Convictions

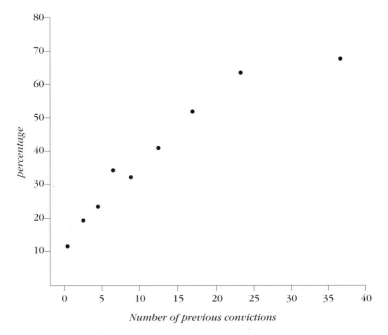

Number of previous convictions

On the basis of such tables and graphs the following factors were seen to be strongly associated with reoffending. For each factor listed, the nature of the association is noted. Further details are presented in the Appendix.

- Age at conviction – risk decreases with age.

- Sex – women reoffend less often than men.

- Employment status at time of offence – greatest risk for those unemployed or in casual jobs, lowest risk for those employed or retired.

- Time in last job – risk decreases the longer the time in last job.

- Marital status at time of release from prison – highest risk for prisoners who are single.

- Type of offence – highest rate of reoffending for theft.

- Age at first conviction – risk decreases with age.

- Number of previous convictions – risk increases with number of previous convictions.

- Number of previous convictions for property offences – risk increases with number of previous convictions for property offences.

- Number of youth custody sentences – risk increases with number of such sentences.

- Number of adult custodial sentences – risk increases with number of such sentences.

- Number of supervision orders – risk increases with number of supervision orders.

More modest degrees of association were found for several other factors, but none of them made a useful contribution to prediction once the factors listed above were taken into account. These other factors included; number of previous probation orders, number of years in full-time education, and number of disciplinary offences whilst in prison.

Prediction scores assume that the influence of each factor is linear, and this needs to be examined. Figure 3.1, for example, shows that the rate of reoffending rises steadily up to about 25 previous convictions and then levels off, offenders with a greater number of previous convictions, summarised by the rightmost point on the graph, showing no greater risk than the last but one group. This suggests that the number of previous convictions should be recoded into the actual number, or 25, whichever is smaller. Several other such recodings were suggested by graphs of this kind.

Although all the factors in the above list were found to be strongly associated with reoffending, many of them are intercorrelated, and a further substantial reduction in the number of factors is possible by taking these correlations into account. This was done by retaining the two-year reoffending horizon and fitting logistic regression models relating the probability of reoffending to various combinations of the factors, checking the resulting coefficients for statistical significance. The importance of each of the factors is nearly always reduced by taking the others into account.

Survival analysis

The central concept in survival analysis is the survival function $S(t)$, defined in this context to be the probability that a prisoner will not reoffend during the period of t days following release. One minus this quantity is the *Risk Function, R(t)*

$$R(t) = \text{Probability (first reoffence occurs within } t \text{ days of release)}$$

The dots in Figure 3.2 show two estimates of $R(t)$, first for any reoffending and second, counting only serious reoffences. As expected, both curves show the risk increasing steadily over time, the curve for serious reoffending being everywhere below that for all reoffending.

A special case of survival modelling, used widely in other applications, is the so-called Weibull model for which

$$R(t) = 1 - \exp(-\lambda t^{\alpha}) \tag{1}$$

Figure 3.2
Percentage Probability of Reoffending

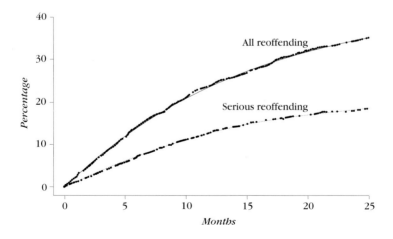

The two parameters of this risk function are λ, which controls the *rate* of reoffending, and α, which controls the *shape* of the dependence of $R(t)$ on the time t. However, Weibull models in this simple form tend not to fit recidivism data very well for the larger values of t, since (1) implies that the prisoner is *bound* to reoffend at some time in the future, as $R(t) \rightarrow 1$ as $t \rightarrow \infty$. A *split population* model assumes that only a proportion p of subjects will reoffend, formula (1) applying only to this segment of the population. The risk function is now

$$R(t) = p(1 - \exp(-\lambda t^{\alpha})).$$

Fitting this model to the data gives a value of α very close to one, with the interpretation that prisoners either never reoffend, with probability $1 - p$, or they reoffend at a constant rate λ. This finding that the shape parameter α is close to 1 has also been noted in earlier studies – see the review and application of survival models in Tarling (1993). Taking $\alpha = 1$ and estimating values of p and λ by fitting this model to the complete sample gave the smooth curves superimposed on Figure 3.2, indicating a very good fit to the data.

The main aim of the analysis was to see how $R(t)$ depends on the values of the various factors specific to each prisoner. Taking $\alpha = 1$, a model which allows this to be done is

$$R_x(t) = p_x(1 - \exp(-\lambda_x t)), \tag{2}$$

where the suffix x on $R(t)$, p and λ show that they all depend on the values of the factors, denoted collectively as x. Since p_x is a probability, the logistic model

$$\log\left(\frac{p_x}{1-p_x}\right) = a_0 + a_1 x_1 + a_2 x_2 + \dots \tag{3}$$

is assumed, where x_1, x_2, ... are the values of a chosen sequence of factors. The fact that the rate parameter λ_x is necessarily positive suggests the log-linear model

$$\log(\lambda_x) = b_0 + b_1 x_1 + b_2 x_2 + \dots \tag{4}$$

The x_is are chosen from the list of selected factors identified in the preliminary analysis.

It is possible to estimate the as and bs in (3) and (4), but it turns out that the standard deviations of the estimates of these coefficients are unacceptably large. Increasing a_0, for instance, increases the proportion of subjects who are in the offending group, whereas increasing b_0 increases the rate of reoffending of those already in the offending group. Both changes have the overall effect of increasing the observed number of reoffences, and are virtually indistinguishable as far as the statistical fit of the model to the data is concerned. Another difficulty with the model is that it requires the evaluation of two functions, both (3) and (4). These difficulties are successfully solved by constraining (3) and (4) to be linear functions of each other, by assuming that

$$\log\left(\frac{p_x}{1 - p_x}\right) = c + d\log \lambda_x.$$

The final model used in the analysis is now summarised by the three equations:

$$R_x(t) = p_x(1 - \exp(-\lambda_x t)) \tag{5}$$

$$\log(\lambda_x) = b_0 + b_1 x_1 + b_2 x_2 + \dots \tag{6}$$

$$\log\left(\frac{p_x}{1 - p_x}\right) = c + db_0 + db_1 x_1 + db_2 x_2 + \dots \tag{7}$$

The parameters in the model were fitted by the method of maximum likelihood. Explicitly, the values of c, d, b_0, b_1, b_2, ... were found which maximise the log-likelihood function

$$\sum_i \{z_i(\log p_i + \log \lambda_i - \lambda t_i) + (1 - z_i) \log(1 - p_i + p_i \exp(-\lambda_i t_i))\} \tag{8}$$

where, for the ith prisoner,

$$t_i = \begin{cases} \text{time in days of first offence if within 2 years} \\ 730 \ \text{otherwise} \end{cases} \tag{9}$$

$$z_i = \begin{cases} 1 \ \text{if } t_i < 730 \\ 0 \ \text{if } t_i = 730 \end{cases} \tag{10}$$

and λ_i, and p_i are the values of (6) and (7) evaluated using the specific factors for the ith prisoner. The maximum likelihood estimates were calculated using the non-linear maximisation routine *nlmin* within the statistical computer package *Splus*.

The ROR

Owing to the small number of women prisoners in the sample, at this stage the model was fitted to the data on the male prisoners only. Several different choices of factors x_i were used in fitting the survival model given by equations (4) to (7). The resulting models were evaluated by examining graphs of the kind to be described below (Figure 3.7), and by testing the statistical significance of the b_i coefficients. The general principle used here was to evaluate the contribution of additional factors by calculating the change in the value of the log-likelihood function (8) brought about by adding these extra coefficients to the model, and then comparing these changes with appropriate percentage points of the χ^2 distribution. Adding squares and products of factors already in the model gives a check for nonlinear terms and interactions.

The final choice for the ROR was to take

$x_1 =$ age at conviction, in years,

$x_2 =$ number of youth custody sentences,

$x_3 =$ number of adult custodial sentences,

$x_4 =$ number of previous convictions (actual number if less than 25, 25 if 25 or over).

The remaining factors x_5 to x_{10} were taken to be dummy variables corresponding to six broad categories for type of offence (namely offences of violence, sexual offences, offences involving drugs, burglary, theft and 'other offences'). For example, x_5 takes the value 1 if the offence is one of violence and 0 otherwise.

The two versions of the ROR were obtained by first defining t_i in (9) to be the time to any reoffence, and secondly counting only serious reoffences.

The resulting scores $b_0 + b_1 x_1 + b_2 x_2 + ...$ can be simplified to make them easier to interpret and use. A scaling factor k was found such that each scaled coefficient $k b_1$, $k b_2$, ... was closer to an integer, which was then rounded to the nearest whole number to give integer weights

$$w_i \approx k b_i.$$

To avoid negative values 100 was added to give the definition of ROR to be

$$ROR = 100 + w_1 x_1 + w_2 x_2 + ...$$

The weights w_1, w_2, ..., w_{10} for the two ROR scores were respectively -1, 2, 3, 1, -1, 1, -8, 4, 8 and -4 for the all reoffences score, and -1, 3, 4, 1, 1, 8, -11, 3, 9 and -10 for the serious reoffences score. These weights will be set out more clearly in Chapter 4 and their use illustrated by examples.

Because of the scaling and rounding used in calculating the weights, the score needs to be calibrated in order to convert the ROR scores into actual estimates of the risk function $R(t)$. This was done by refitting the survival model but using ROR as if it was a single x factor. This procedure finds values of C, D, B_0 and B_1 so that

$$R(t) = p(1 - \exp(-\lambda t)) \tag{11}$$

where now

$$\log(\lambda) = B_0 + B_1 \times ROR \tag{12}$$

and

$$\log\left(\frac{p}{1-p}\right) = C + DB_0 + DB_1 \times ROR \tag{13}$$

The fitting procedure is exactly the same as in (8) to (10), except that the values of λ_i and p_i are given by calculating (12) and (13) using the ROR score for the ith prisoner.

The estimates of the quantities (C, D, B_0, B_1) for the two versions of the ROR are as follows:

Coefficient	Any reoffending	Serious reoffending
C	11.6	11.7
D	1.74	1.97
B_0	-9.17	-8.55
B_1	0.0293	0.0215

The value of the risk for any male prisoner and for any time t is now obtained by calculating ROR and substituting its value into (12) and (13), and thence into (11). This calculation is most easily done by using a table showing the values of $R(t)$ for a range of values of t and a range of values of ROR. These tables, one for all reoffending and one for serious reoffending, are set out in Appendix B, and their use illustrated by examples in Chapter 4.

Values of ROR vary widely across the prisoners in the sample. The histogram of ROR for all reoffences is shown in Figure 3.3, and that for serious reoffences in Figure 3.4.

Figure 3.3
Scores for all reoffending

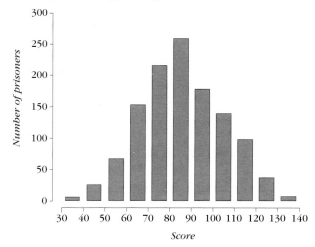

Figure 3.4
Scores for serious reoffending

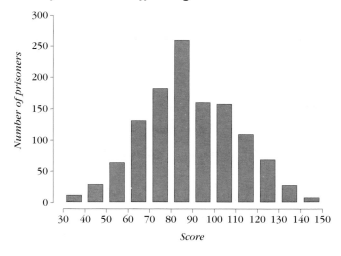

Each value of ROR converts into an estimate of risk at two years, $R(730)$. The corresponding histograms of these risk estimates are in Figures 3.5 and 3.6.

Figure 3.5
Histogram of risk: all reoffending, 2 years

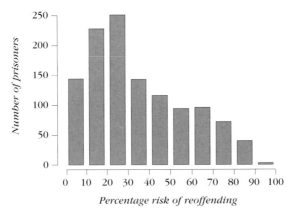

Percentage risk of reoffending

Figure 3.6
Histogram of risk: serious reoffending, 2 years

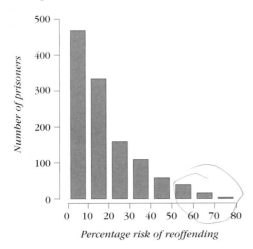

Percentage risk of reoffending

As expected both these distributions are strongly skewed to the right; a relatively large number of prisoners having a low risk and a relatively small number of prisoners having a high risk. In only a small number of cases is the ROR able to predict a probability of serious reoffending of more than 50 per cent in two years.

The statistical fit of the survival model for all reoffending is shown in Figure 3.7.

Figure 3.7
Percentage probability of any reoffending, by risk group

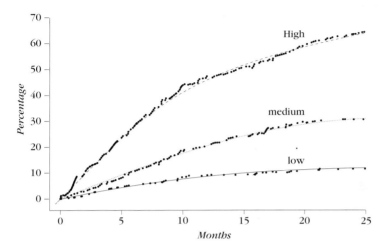

Here the values of ROR were calculated for all prisoners, and three groups of cases selected, those with the lowest 20% of scores, those with the middle 20% of scores, and those with the highest 20% of scores. These represent low risk, medium risk and high risk cases respectively. The dots in the graph show the empirical risk functions calculated directly from the data, using the pattern of reoffending observed in each of these three groups. The smooth curves in Figure 3.7 are the values of $R(t)$ calculated from the model, after averaging over the estimated risk functions for the prisoners in each group. They give a very good fit. A similar graph is obtained for the serious reoffending model.

As mentioned, the ROR was fitted to the data on the male prisoners only, as the number of women with sentences of four years or more was far too few to enable the full survival model to be fitted to the female prisoners separately. Applying the ROR formula as it is to the 55 women in the sample predicts that about 10 of them will reoffend within two years, of whom about four are expected to commit serious offences. The actual number reoffending in two years was five, of whom four committed serious offences. This suggests that the risk for women is smaller than that for men for all reoffending but about the same for serious reoffending, although the numbers are too small to be certain. A much restricted version of the survival model was fitted to the data for the women only, constraining all the parameters to take the same values as before except for a single sex adjustment S given by:

$$ROR_{female} = ROR_{male} + S$$

The estimated values of S are -13 for all reoffending and -1 for serious reoffending. This allows ROR to be calculated for both men and women, but the resulting risk estimates for women can only be taken as a very rough guide to the likely pattern of their reoffending.

4 The practical application of Risk of Reconviction (ROR)

The analysis described in the previous chapter led to the Risk of Reconviction (ROR) being constructed from the following six items of information, all of which are available at the time the current sentence is imposed:

1. age at conviction (the conviction for which the prospective parolee is currently serving his or her sentence)

2. number of youth custody sentences (including current sentence)

3. number of adult custodial sentences (including current sentence)

4. number of previous convictions (actual number if less than 25, 25 if 25 or over)

5. type of offence for which serving current sentence, in six broad categories: offences of violence; sex offences; drugs offences; burglary; theft, fraud and forgery; and other offences

6. whether male or female.

The complex coefficients and functions presented in the previous chapter can be readily converted to simple weights which can be combined to predict a 'score' for any individual. From the score the probability or risk of reoffending can be calculated, for lengths of parole varying from one to twenty-four months. Two scores, and hence two estimates of risk are produced: one to estimate the risk of any reoffending (apart from most summary and minor motoring offences), the second to estimate serious reoffending which is taken as offending resulting in a further custodial sentence. The weights are set out in Table 4.1.

Table 4.1
Weights for the variable used to calculate the prediction scores

(Start with 100)

| | Weights | |
| | Any | Serious |
Variable	reoffending	reoffending
1. Age at conviction	-1	-1
2. Number of youth custody sentences	+3	+4
3. Number of adult custodial sentences	+2	+3
4. Number of previous convictions (actual number if less than 25, 25 if 25 or over)		
5. Offence type:		
violence	-1	+1
sexual	+1	+8
drugs	-8	-11
burglary	+4	+3
theft	+8	+9
other	-4	-10
6. If female	-13	-1

The value for each variable is multiplied by the relevant weight and the result-ing totals added. One hundred is then added to this total to produce the final score. Having derived the score the probability of any reoffending is given in Table B.1 of Appendix B and the probability of serious reoffending is given in Table B.2 of Appendix B. The scores are shown as the columns of Tables B.1 and B.2 and the rows give the number of months following release. For any given score and for any time following release ("parole window") the cell of the table shows the percentage probability of reoffending.

It is important to restate that the predictor does not produce an individual prediction but represents the proportion of the sample who reoffended, and is an average rate for prisoners matched on the variable listed in Table 4.1. In individual cases other factors known to the Parole Board will also be relevant.

As described in more detail in the previous chapter, the prediction score was estimated from the information available only for the men in the sample. Too few women were sentenced for a detailed calculation to be made separately. Instead, an approximate prediction score was calculated for women, adjust-ing that for men by using the approximate relationship between female and male reoffending amongst those released in 1987. Inevitably the score for women provides a less certain guide to risk. The adjustment to the score for female prisoners is given in Table 4.1.

Examples

To illustrate how the scores are calculated and used in practice, two examples are given below.

Example 1

A male prisoner aged 20 at the time of conviction, with 13 previous convictions, of which two resulted in youth custody sentences who is serving a sentence for a theft offence.

This man has a score for any reoffending of 110. It is calculated as follows:

Variable			Weight	Score
1. age at conviction	=	20	-1	-1 x 20 = -20
2. number of youth custody sentences	=	3	+3	+3 x 3 = +9
3. number of adult custodial sentences	=	0	+2	+2 x 0 = 0
4. number of previous convictions	=	13	+1	+1 x 13 = +13
5. offence type	=	theft	+8	+8 = +8
6. sex	=	male	0	0
Total score				+10
Final score = total score + 100				+110

From Table B.1, a score of 110 gives a reoffending probability (for any offence) of 48 per cent within the first year (see row 12) and 67 per cent within two years (see row 24). For serious reoffending, then (using the appropriate weights in Table 4.1 and the figures in Table B.2), the score becomes 114 which gives a probability of serious reoffending within a year of 24 per cent and 35 per cent within two years.

Example 2

A male prisoner aged 39 at time of conviction, with no previous convictions (and thus no prior custodial sentences, either youth or adult) with an offence of violence.

This man has a score predicting any reoffending as follows:

Variable			Weight	Score
1. age at conviction	=	39	-1	-1 x 39 = -39
2. number of youth custody sentences	=	0	+3	+3 x 0 = 0
3. number of adult custodial sentences	=	1	+2	+2 x 1 = +2
4. number of previous convictions	=	0	+1	+1 x 0 = 0
5. offence type	=	violence	-1	-1 = -1
6. sex	=	male	0	0
Total score				-38
Final score = total score + 100				+62

From Table B.1, a score of 62 gives a reoffending probability (for any offence) of five per cent within the first year and nine per cent within two years. For serious reoffending, then (using the appropriate weights in Table 4.1 and the figures in Table B.2), the score becomes 65 which gives a probability of serious reoffending within a year of two per cent and four per cent within two years.

An alternative way of looking at these results is to set them out as 'probability curves', i.e. curves which represent the probability of reoffending during any specified period after discharge for offenders with these particular scores. This is done in Figure 4.1 – both for any reoffending and for serious reoffending. The probability curves are, in fact, the probabilities shown in the appropriate columns of Tables B.1 and B.2.

Figure 4.1
Probability of reoffending during specified period

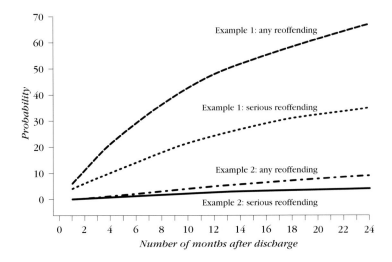

The predictor is now in operation. A computer programme has been developed which enables the Parole Board Secretariat to calculate the score for each parole-elegible prisoner, that is, all prisoners sentenced to four years or more since 1 October 1992. A page is included in the dossier disclosed to the prisoner, setting out his Risk of Reconviction for the two outcomes. A copy is also included in the papers sent to Parole Board members reviewing the case and is shown at Appendix C; the fictional prisoner is the one described in the case study 'Example 1'.

Future developments

It is worth noting that the study could only hope to simulate the effect of the new arrangements, as the prisoners in the sample were either released under previous parole arrangements, or had served out their full sentence (minus remission). Currently offenders are released to supervision at the three-quarters point of their sentence and remain 'at risk' (of serving out the remainder of their sentence in prison) until the end of sentence. If there is a supervision or parole effect on reoffending, then these new arrangements (with their element of compulsory supervision), may result in lower rates of reoffending, at least during the supervision and/or 'at risk' periods.

Thus, it may well be that at some point in the future the predictor will need to be revalidated on a sample of prisoners released under the Criminal Justice Act 1991 arrangements, although it will be some considerable time before a representative sample of people discharged from sentences of four years and over can be built up.

Appendix A - Risk factor by number and percentage reoffending within two years

Age at conviction[1]

	Number	Percentage reoffending any reoffending	Percentage reoffending serious reoffending
13 to 17	30	53	23
18 to 20	136	46	30
21 to 24	246	45	23
25 to 29	287	37	17
30 to 39	339	27	14
40 to 49	150	17	10
50 and over	54	9	4
Total	1,242[2]	34	18

1.   Analysis used age at conviction as a continuous variable.
2.   In four cases age of conviction was not recorded.

Sex

	Number	Percentage reoffending any reoffending	Percentage reoffending serious reoffending
Male	1,191	35	18
Female	55	9	7
Total	1,246	34	18

Employment status at time of offence

	Number	Percentage reoffending any reoffending	Percentage reoffending serious reoffending
Employed/self-employed or casual	414	19	9
Unemployed	722	41	22
Other/retired	29	24	7
No information	81	43	21
Total	1,246	34	18

Time in last job

	Number	Percentage reoffending any reoffending	Percentage reoffending serious reoffending
5 years or more	115	13	3
3 years < 5 years	85	15	6
1 year < 3 years	158	29	13
6 months < 12 months	87	23	10
1 month < 6 months	97	41	24
< 1 month	26	35	19
Casual/several short jobs	100	46	20
No work since last release	18	72	39
No work for five years or more	53	57	32
Does not apply/ does not normally work	50	42	24
No information	457	37	21
Total	1,246	34	18

Marital status at time of release from prison

	Number	Percentage reoffending any reoffending	Percentage reoffending serious reoffending
Married/separated/ divorced/widowed	580	25	12
Single	640	42	23
No information	26	39	15
Total	1,246	34	18

Type of offence

	Number	Percentage reoffending any reoffending	Percentage reoffending serious reoffending
Violence	552	34	18
Sexual	149	30	17
Drugs	147	16	6
Burglary	203	55	29
Theft	89	30	18
Other	105	28	10
Total	1,245[1]	34	18

1.   In one case type of offence was not recorded.

Age at first conviction

	Number	Percentage reoffending any reoffending	Percentage reoffending serious reoffending
Under 13	161	54	30
13 to 17	474	45	22
18 to 20	142	26	15
21 to 24	133	25	14
25 to 29	125	19	9
30 to 39	127	12	7
40 to 49	50	12	0
50 and over	27	4	4
Total	1,239[1]	34	18

1.   In seven cases age at first conviction was not recorded.

Number of previous convictions[1]

	Number	Percentage reoffending any reoffending	Percentage reoffending serious reoffending
None	213	8	4
1	133	19	7
2	123	21	10
3 to 4	190	29	12
5 to 6	143	39	22
7 to 9	175	45	23
10 to 14	178	55	29
15 to 19	69	70	45
20 to 24	16	81	56
25 or more	6	83	33
Total	1,246	34	18

1.   Analysis used number of previous convictions as a continuous variable.

Number of previous convictions for property offences

	Number	Percentage reoffending any reoffending	Percentage reoffending serious reoffending
None	289	12	5
1	107	17	6
2	112	28	14
3	108	26	8
4	86	28	15
5	75	41	20
6	61	56	33
7	70	41	26
8	42	55	33
9 or more	289	57	32
Total	1,239[1]	34	18

1. In seven cases number of previous convictions for property offences was not recorded.

Number of youth custody sentences

	Number	Percentage reoffending any reoffending	Percentage reoffending serious reoffending
None	753	20	9
1	173	39	22
2 to 3	210	55	27
4 to 7	104	74	47
8 or more	6	100	83
Total	1,246	34	18

Number of adult custodial sentences

	Number	Percentage reoffending any reoffending	Percentage reoffending serious reoffending
None	744	27	13
1	191	33	19
2 to 3	187	42	23
4 to 7	99	65	38
8 or more	25	48	36
Total	1,246	34	18

Number of supervision orders

	Number	Percentage reoffending any reoffending	Percentage reoffending serious reoffending
None	987	29	15
1	201	50	24
2 or more	55	55	36
Total	1,243[1]	34	18

1.   In three cases number of supervision orders was not recorded.

Appendix B - Probability of reoffending by risk score and time following release

Appendix B

Table B.1: Percentage probability of reoffending (any reoffence), by month following discharge

Reconviction prediction score

No of months following release	60	62	65	70	75	80	85	90	94	96	98	100	101	102	103	104	105	106	107	108	109	110	115	120	125	130	135	140	145	150	155	160
1	0	0	1	1	1	1	2	2	3	3	4	4	4	4	4	5	5	5	5	6	6	6	7	9	10	12	14	17	19	22	25	29
2	1	1	1	1	2	3	4	5	6	6	7	8	8	8	9	9	9	10	10	11	11	12	14	16	19	23	26	30	34	39	44	49
3	1	1	2	2	3	4	5	7	9	9	10	11	12	12	13	13	14	14	15	15	16	17	20	24	27	32	36	41	47	52	58	63
4	2	2	2	3	4	5	7	9	11	12	13	14	15	16	16	17	18	18	19	20	21	21	25	30	35	40	45	51	56	62	68	73
5	2	2	3	4	5	7	9	11	14	15	16	18	18	19	20	21	21	22	23	24	25	26	30	35	41	47	52	58	64	70	75	81
6	2	3	3	4	6	8	10	13	16	17	19	20	21	22	23	24	25	26	27	28	29	30	35	41	46	52	59	65	70	76	81	86
7	3	3	4	5	6	8	12	15	18	20	21	23	24	25	26	27	28	29	30	31	32	33	39	45	51	58	64	70	75	81	85	89
8	3	3	4	6	8	9	13	17	20	22	24	26	27	28	29	30	31	32	33	35	36	37	43	49	56	62	68	74	79	84	88	92
9	3	4	5	6	8	10	15	19	22	24	26	28	29	30	32	33	34	35	36	38	39	40	46	53	59	66	72	78	83	87	91	94
10	4	4	5	7	9	11	16	20	24	26	28	31	32	33	34	35	37	38	39	40	42	43	50	56	63	69	75	81	85	89	92	95
11	4	5	6	8	10	12	17	22	26	28	30	33	34	35	36	38	39	40	42	43	44	46	52	59	66	72	78	83	87	91	94	96
12	4	5	6	9	11	13	18	23	28	30	32	35	36	37	39	40	41	43	44	45	47	48	55	62	68	75	80	85	89	92	95	96
13	5	5	6	9	12	14	20	25	29	32	34	37	38	39	41	42	43	45	46	48	49	50	57	64	71	77	82	87	90	93	95	97
14	5	6	7	10	12	15	21	26	31	33	36	39	40	41	43	44	45	47	48	50	51	53	60	66	73	79	84	88	91	94	96	97
15	5	6	7	10	13	16	22	27	32	35	37	40	42	43	44	46	47	49	50	52	53	54	62	68	75	80	85	89	92	94	96	97
16	6	6	8	11	14	17	23	29	34	36	39	42	43	45	46	48	49	50	52	53	55	56	63	70	76	82	86	90	93	95	96	97
17	6	7	8	11	14	18	24	30	35	38	41	43	45	46	48	49	51	52	54	55	57	58	65	72	78	83	87	91	93	95	97	98
18	6	7	8	12	15	19	25	31	36	39	42	45	46	48	49	51	52	54	55	57	58	59	67	73	79	84	88	91	94	96	97	98
19	6	7	9	12	16	20	26	32	37	40	43	46	48	49	51	52	54	55	57	58	60	61	68	74	80	85	89	92	94	96	97	98
20	7	8	9	12	16	20	27	33	39	40	44	47	49	50	52	53	55	56	58	59	61	62	69	75	81	86	89	92	94	96	97	98
21	7	8	10	13	16	20	28	34	40	43	46	49	50	52	53	55	56	58	59	61	62	63	70	77	82	86	90	93	95	96	97	98
22	7	8	10	13	17	21	28	35	41	44	47	50	51	53	54	56	57	59	60	62	63	65	71	77	83	87	90	93	95	96	97	98
23	8	9	10	14	18	23	29	36	42	45	48	51	52	54	55	57	58	60	61	63	64	66	72	78	83	87	91	93	95	96	97	98
24	8	9	11	14	19	24	30	37	43	46	49	52	53	55	56	58	59	61	62	64	65	67	73	79	84	88	91	93	95	96	97	98

Example 2

Example 1

Table B.2: Percentage probability of reoffending (serious offences), by month following discharge

Reconviction prediction score

No of months following release	60	65	70	75	80	85	90	92	94	96	98	99	100	101	105	106	107	108	109	110	114	115	120	125	130	135	140	145
1	0	0	0	0	0	1	1	1	1	1	1	1	1	2	2	2	2	2	2	2	3	3	4	5	6	7	8	9
2	0	0	1	1	1	1	2	2	2	2	3	3	3	3	4	4	4	4	4	5	6	6	7	9	11	13	15	17
3	0	1	1	1	1	2	2	3	3	3	4	4	4	4	5	6	6	6	6	7	8	8	10	13	15	18	21	24
4	1	1	1	1	2	2	3	4	4	4	4	5	5	6	7	7	8	8	8	9	10	11	13	16	19	23	26	30
5	1	1	1	2	2	3	4	4	5	5	6	6	7	7	8	9	9	10	10	11	12	13	16	19	23	27	31	36
6	1	1	2	2	3	4	5	5	6	6	7	7	8	8	10	10	11	11	12	12	14	15	18	22	26	31	36	41
7	1	1	2	2	3	4	5	6	7	7	8	8	9	9	11	12	12	13	13	14	16	17	21	25	29	34	39	45
8	1	2	2	3	4	5	6	7	7	8	9	9	10	10	12	13	14	14	15	15	18	19	23	27	32	37	43	48
9	1	2	2	3	4	5	7	8	8	9	10	10	11	11	14	14	15	15	16	17	20	21	25	30	35	40	46	52
10	1	2	3	3	4	6	7	9	9	10	11	11	12	12	15	15	16	17	17	18	21	22	27	32	37	43	49	54
11	2	2	3	4	5	6	8	9	10	10	11	12	13	13	16	16	17	18	19	19	23	24	28	34	39	45	51	57
12	2	2	3	4	5	6	8	9	11	11	12	13	13	14	17	18	18	19	20	21	24	25	30	35	41	47	53	59
13	2	2	3	4	5	7	9	10	11	12	13	14	14	15	18	18	19	20	21	22	25	26	31	37	43	49	55	61
14	2	2	3	4	6	7	9	10	12	12	14	14	15	16	19	19	20	21	22	23	27	28	33	38	44	50	57	62
15	2	3	4	5	6	8	10	11	12	13	14	15	16	16	19	20	21	22	23	24	28	29	34	40	46	52	58	64
16	2	3	4	5	6	8	10	11	13	14	15	16	16	17	20	21	22	23	24	25	29	30	35	41	47	53	59	65
17	2	3	4	5	7	8	11	12	13	14	16	16	17	18	21	22	23	24	25	26	30	31	36	42	48	54	60	66
18	2	3	4	5	7	9	11	12	14	15	16	17	18	18	22	23	24	24	25	26	31	32	37	43	49	55	61	67
19	2	3	4	5	7	9	12	13	14	16	17	18	19	19	22	23	25	25	26	27	31	33	38	44	50	56	62	68
20	3	3	4	6	8	9	12	13	15	16	18	19	19	20	23	24	25	26	27	28	32	34	39	45	51	57	63	69
21	3	4	5	6	8	10	12	14	15	16	18	19	20	21	24	25	26	27	28	29	33	34	40	46	52	58	64	69
22	3	4	5	6	8	10	13	14	15	17	18	19	20	21	24	25	26	27	28	29	34	35	41	47	53	59	65	70
23	3	4	5	6	8	10	13	14	16	17	19	20	20	21	25	26	27	28	29	30	34	35	41	47	53	59	65	70
24	3	4	5	6	8	11	13	15	16	18	19	20	21	22	25	26	27	28	29	30	35	36	42	48	54	60	66	71

Example 2 (columns 65–70)

Example 1 (columns 114–115)

Appendix C - Risk of Reconviction

Name : Example 1

Sex : Male

Parole number : P999

Risk of Reconviction

The Risk of Reconviction is estimated from the past offending records of a very large number of prisoners. It is the percentage of released prisoners with similar offending records who have committed further offences within a particular time. It is based on the criminal record below. The Parole Board of course takes account of much other information in assessing the risk of reoffending by an individual prisoner.

Age when convicted (years)	20
Number of youth custody sentences (not counting current one)	2
Number of adult custody sentences (not counting current one)	0
Number of previous convictions	13
Offence type	Theft

This information results in calculated scores of:

Risk of Reconviction (%) for any offending by the end of:

Month	1	2	3	4	5	6	7	8	9	10	11	12
%	6	12	17	21	26	30	33	37	40	43	46	48
Month	13	14	15	16	17	18	19	20	21	22	23	24
%	50	53	54	56	58	59	61	62	63	65	66	67

Risk of Reconviction (%) for serious offending (resulting in a custodial sentence) by the end of:

Month	1	2	3	4	5	6	7	8	9	10	11	12
%	3	6	8	10	12	14	16	18	20	21	23	24
Month	13	14	15	16	17	18	19	20	21	22	23	24
%	25	27	28	29	30	31	31	32	33	34	34	35

References

Carlisle, Rt Hon Lord of Bucklow, **(1988).** *The Parole System in England and Wales.* **Report of the Review Committee.** London:HMSO.

Copas, J.B., Ditchfield, J. and Marshall, P. (1994). Development of a new reconviction predictor score. *Research Bulletin No 36.* London: Home Office Research and Statistics Directorate.

Farrington, D.P. and Tarling, R. (1985). *Prediction in Criminology.* Albany, New York : SUNY.

Nuttall, C.P. *et al* (1977). *Parole in England and Wales.* **Home Office Research Study No 38.** London : HMSO.

Pease, K. (1988). *Judgements of Crime Seriousness.* **Research and Planning Unit Paper No 44.** London : Home Office Research and Statistics Directorate.

Schmidt, P. and Witte, A.D. (1988). *Predicting Recidivism Using Survival Models.* New York : Springer-Verlog.

Tarling, R. (1993). *Analysing Offending: Data, Models and Interpretations.* London : HMSO.

Ward, D. (1987). *The Validity of the Reconviction Prediction Score.* **Home Office Research Study No 94.** London : HMSO.

Publications

List of Research and Statistics Directorate (formerly Research and Planning Unit) Publications

The Research and Statistics Directorate has been publishing its work since 1955, and a list of reports for the last three years is provided below. A **full** list of publications is available on request from the Research and Statistics Directorate Information Section.

Home Office Research Studies (HORS)

125. **Magistrates' court or Crown Court? Mode of trial decisions and sentencing.** Carol Hedderman and David Moxon. 1992. vii + 53pp. (0 11 341036 0).

126. **Developments in the use of compensation orders in magistrates' courts since October 1988.** David Moxon, John Martin Corkery and Carol Hedderman. 1992. x + 48pp. (0 11 341042 5).

127. **A comparative study of firefighting arrangements in Britain, Denmark, The Netherlands and Sweden.** John Graham, Simon Field, Roger Tarling and Heather Wilkinson. 1992. x + 57pp. (0 11 341043 3).

128. **The National Prison Survey 1991: main findings.** Roy Walmsley, Liz Howard and Sheila White. 1992. xiv + 82pp. (0 11 341051 4).

129. **Changing the Code: police detention under the revised PACE Codes of Practice.** David Brown, Tom Ellis and Karen Larcombe. 1992. viii + 122pp. (0 11 341052 2).

130. **Car theft: the offender's perspective.** Roy Light, Claire Nee and Helen Ingham. 1993. x + 89pp. (0 11 341069 7).

131. **Housing, Community and Crime: The Impact of the Priority Estates Project.** Janet Foster, Timothy Hope with assistance from Lizanne Dowds and Mike Sutton. 1993. xi + 118pp (0 11 341078).

132. **The 1992 British Crime Survey.** Pat Mayhew, Natalie Aye Maung and Catriona Mirrlees-Black. 1993. xiii + 206pp. (0 11 341094 8).

133. **Intensive Probation in England and Wales: an evaluation.** George Mair, Charles Lloyd, Claire Nee and Rae Sibbett. 1994. xiv + 143pp. (0 11 341114 6).

134. **Contacts between Police and Public: findings from the 1992 British Crime Survey.** Wesley G Skogan. 1995. ix + 93pp. (0 11 341115 4).

135. **Policing low-level disorder : Police use of Section 5 of the Public Order Act 1986.** David Brown and Tom Ellis. 1994. ix + 69pp. (0 11 341116 2).

136. **Explaining reconviction rates: A critical analysis.** Charles Lloyd, George Mair and Mike Hough. 1995. xiv + 103pp. (0 11 341117 0).

137. **Case Screening by the Crown Prosecution Service: How and why cases are terminated.** Debbie Crisp and David Moxon. 1995. viii + 66pp. (0 11 341137 5).

138. **Public Interest Case Assessment Schemes.** Debbie Crisp, Claire Whittaker and Jessica Harris. 1995. x + 58pp. (0 11 341139 1).

139. **Policing domestic violence in the 1990s.** Sharon Grace. 1995. x + 74pp. (0 11 341140 5).

140. **Young people, victimisation and the police: British Crime Survey findings on experiences and attitudes of 12 to 15 year olds.** Natalie Aye Maung. xii + 140pp. (Not yet published)

141. **The Settlement of refugees in Britain.** Jenny Carey-Wood, Karen Duke, Valerie Karn and Tony Marshall. 1995. xii + 133pp. (0 11 341145 6).

142. **Vietnamese Refugees since 1982.** Karen Duke and Tony Marshall. 1995. x + 62pp. (0 11 341147 2).

143. **The Parish Special Constables Scheme.** Peter Southgate, Tom Bucke and Carole Byron. 1995. x + 59pp. (1 85893 458 3).

144. **Measuring the Satisfaction of the Courts with the Probation Service.** Chris May. 1995. x + 76pp. (1 85893 483 4).

145. **Young people and crime.** John Graham and Benjamin Bowling. 1995. 142pp. (1 85893 551 2).

146. **Crime against retail and manufacturing premises: findings from the 1994 Commercial Victimisation Survey.** Catriona Mirrlees-Black and Alec Ross. 1995. xi + 110pp. (1 85893 554 7).

147. **Anxiety about crime: findings from the 1994 British Crime Survey.** Michael Hough. 1995. viii + 92pp. (1 85893 553 9).

Research and Planning Unit Papers (RPUP)

65. **Offending while on bail: a survey of recent studies.** Patricia M. Morgan. 1992.

66. **Juveniles sentenced for serious offences: a comparison of regimes in Young Offender Institutions and Local Authority Community Homes.** John Ditchfield and Liza Catan. 1992.

67. **The management and deployment of police armed response vehicles.** Peter Southgate. 1992.

68. **Using psychometric personality tests in the selection of firearms officers.** Catriona Mirrlees-Black. 1992.

69. **Bail information schemes: practice and effect.** Charles Lloyd. 1992.

70. **Crack and cocaine in England and Wales**. Joy Mott (editor). 1992.

71. **Rape: from recording to conviction.** Sharon Grace, Charles Lloyd and Lorna J. F. Smith. 1992.

72. **The National Probation Survey 1990.** Chris May. 1993.

73. **Public satisfaction with police services.** Peter Southgate and Debbie Crisp. 1993.

74. **Disqualification from driving: an effective penalty?** Catriona Mirrlees-Black. 1993.

75. **Detention under the Prevention of Terrorism (Temporary Provisions) Act 1989: Access to legal advice and outside contact.** David Brown. 1993.

76. **Panel assessment schemes for mentally disordered offenders.** Carol Hedderman. 1993.

77. **Cash-limiting the probation service: a case study in resource allocation.** Simon Field and Mike Hough. 1993.

78. **The probation response to drug misuse.** Claire Nee and Rae Sibbitt. 1993.

79 **Approval of rifle and target shooting clubs: the effects of the new and revised criteria.** John Martin Corkery. 1993.

80. **The long-term needs of victims: A review of the literature.** Tim Newburn. 1993.

81. **The welfare needs of unconvicted prisoners.** Diane Caddle and Sheila White. 1994.

82. **Racially motivated crime: a British Crime Survey analysis.** Natalie Aye Maung and Catriona Mirrlees-Black. 1994.

83. **Mathematical models for forecasting Passport demand.** Andy Jones and John MacLeod. 1994.

84. **The theft of firearms**. John Corkery. 1994.

85. **Equal opportunities and the Fire Service.** Tom Bucke. 1994.

86. **Drug Education Amongst Teenagers: a 1992 British Crime Survey Analysis**. Lizanne Dowds and Judith Redfern. 1995.

87. **Group 4 Prisoner Escort Service: a survey of customer satisfaction.** Claire Nee. 1994.

88. **Special Considerations: Issues for the Management and Organisation of the Volunteer Police.** Catriona Mirrlees-Black and Carole Byron. 1995.

89. **Self-reported drug misuse in England and Wales: findings from the 1992 British Crime Survey.** Joy Mott and Catriona Mirrlees-Black. 1995.

90. **Improving bail decisions: the bail process project, phase 1.**
John Burrows, Paul Henderson and Patricia Morgan. 1995.

91. **Practitioners' views of the Criminal Justice Act: a survey of criminal justice agencies.** George Mair and Chris May. 1995.

92. **Obscene, threatening and other troublesome telephone calls to women in England and Wales: 1982-1992.** Wendy Buck, Michael Chatterton and Ken Pease. 1995.

93. **A survey of the prisoner escort and custody service provided by Group 4 and by Securicor Custodial Services.** Diane Caddle. 1995.

Research Findings

1. **Magistrates' court or Crown Court? Mode of trial decisions and their impact on sentencing.** Carol Hedderman and David Moxon. 1992.

2. **Surveying crime: findings from the 1992 British Crime Survey.** Pat Mayhew and Natalie Aye Maung. 1992.

3. **Car Theft: the offenders' perspective.** Claire Nee. 1993.

4. **The National Prison Survey 1991: main findings.** Roy Walmsley, Liz Howard and Sheila White. 1993.

5. **Changing the Code: Police detention under the revised PACE codes of practice.** David Brown, Tom Ellis and Karen Larcombe. 1993.

6. **Rifle and pistol target shooting clubs: The effects of new approval criteria.** John M. Corkery. 1993.

7. **Self-reported drug misuse in England and Wales. Main findings from the 1992 British Crime Survey.** Joy Mott and Catriona Mirrlees-Black. 1993.

8. **Findings from the International Crime Survey.** Pat Mayhew. 1994.

9 **Fear of Crime: Findings from the 1992 British Crime Survey.** Catriona Mirrlees-Black and Natalie Aye Maung. 1994.

10.   **Does the Criminal Justice system treat men and women differently?** Carol Hedderman and Mike Hough. 1994.

11.   **Participation in Neighbourhood Watch: Findings from the 1992 British Crime Survey.** Lizanne Dowds and Pat Mayhew. 1994.

12.   **Explaining Reconviction Rates: A Critical Analysis.** Charles Lloyd, George Mair and Mike Hough. 1995.

13.   **Equal opportunities and the Fire Service.** Tom Bucke. 1994.

14.   **Trends in Crime: Findings from the 1994 British Crime Survey.** Pat Mayhew, Catriona Mirrlees-Black and Natalie Aye Maung. 1994.

15.   **Intensive Probation in England and Wales: an evaluation.** George Mair, Charles Lloyd, Claire Nee and Rae Sibbett. 1995.

16.   **The settlement of refugees in Britain.** Jenny Carey-Wood, Karen Duke, Valerie Karn and Tony Marshall. 1995.

17.   **Young people, victimisation and the police: British Crime Survey findings on experiences and attitudes of 12 to 15 year olds.** Natalie Aye Maung. (Not yet published)

18.   **Vietnamese Refugees since 1982.** Karen Duke and Tony Marshall. 1995.

19.   **Supervision of Restricted Patients in the Community.** Dell and Grounds. (Not yet published)

20.   **Videotaping children's evidence: an evaluation.** Graham Davies, Clare Wilson, Rebecca Mitchell and John Milsom. 1995.

21.   **The mentally disordered and the police.** Graham Robertson, Richard Pearson and Robert Gibb. 1995.

22.   **Preparing records of taped interviews.** Andrew Hooke and Jim Knox. 1995.

23.   **Obscene, threating and other troublesome telephone calls to women: Findings from the British Crime Survey.** Wendy Buck, Michael Chatterton and Ken Pease. 1995.

24. **Young people and crime.** John Graham and Ben Bowling. 1995.

25. **Anxiety about crime: Findings from the 1994 British Crime Survey.** Michael Hough. 1995.

26. **Crime against retail premises in 1993.** Catriona Mirrlees-Black and Alec Ross. 1995.

27. **Crime against manufacturing premises in 1993.** Catriona Mirrlees-Black and Alec Ross. 1995.

Research Bulletin

The Research Bulletin is published twice each year and contains short articles on recent research. Research Bulletin No. 37 was the most recent to be published.

Occasional Papers

Coping with a crisis: the introduction of three and two in a cell. T. G. Weiler. 1992.

Psychiatric Assessment at the Magistrates' Court. Philip Joseph. 1992.

Measurement of caseload weightings in magistrates' courts. Richard J. Gadsden and Graham J. Worsdale. 1992.

The CDE of scheduling in magistrates' courts. John W. Raine and Michael J. Willson. 1992.

Employment opportunities for offenders. David Downes. 1993.

Sex offenders: a framework for the evaluation of community-based treatment. Mary Barker and Rod Morgan. 1993.

Suicide attempts and self-injury in male prisons. Alison Liebling and Helen Krarup. 1993.

Measurement of caseload weightings associated with the Children Act. Richard J. Gadsden and Graham J. Worsdale. 1994. (Available from the RSD Information Section.)

Managing difficult prisoners: The Lincoln and Hull special units. Professor Keith Bottomley, Professor Norman Jepson, Mr Kenneth Elliott and Dr Jeremy Coid. 1994. (Available from RSD Information Section.)

The Nacro diversion initiative for mentally disturbed offenders: an account and an evaluation. Home Office, NACRO and Mental Health Foundation. 1994. (Available from RSD Information Section.)

Probation Motor Projects in England and Wales. J P Martin and Douglas Martin. 1994.

Community-based treatment of sex offenders: an evaluation of seven treatment programmes. R Beckett, A Beech, D Fisher and A S Fordham. 1994.

Videotaping children's evidence: an evaluation. Graham Davies, Clare Wilson, Rebecca Mitchell and John Milsom. 1995.

Managing the needs of female prisoners. Allison Morris, Chris Wilkinson, Andrea Tisi, Jane Woodrow and Ann Rockley. 1995.

Local information points for volunteers. Michael Locke, Nick Richards, Lorraine Down, Jon Griffish and Roger Worgan. 1995.

Books

Analysing Offending. Data, Models and Interpretations. Roger Tarling. 1993. viii + 203pp. (0 11 341080 8).

Requests for Publications

Home Office Research Studies from 143 onwards, *Research and Planning Unit Papers, Research Findings, the Research and Planning Unit Programme and Research Bulletins* are available on request from the Information Section, Home Office Research and Statistics Directorate, Room 278, 50 Queen Anne's Gate, London SW1H 9AT. Telephone: 0171 273 2084 (answering machine).

Occasional Papers can be purchased from: Home Office, Publications Unit, 50 Queen Anne's Gate, London SW1H 9AT. Telephone: 0171 273 2302.

Home Office Research Studies prior to 143 can be purchased from:

HMSO Publications Centre

(Mail, fax and telephone orders only)
PO Box 276, London SW8 5DT
Telephone orders: 0171-873 9090
General enquiries: 0171-873 0011
(queuing system in operation for both numbers)
Fax orders: 0171-873 8200

*And also from **HMSO Bookshops***

FURTHER COPIES OF THIS REPORT ARE AVAILABLE FROM:
INFORMATION SECTION
HOME OFFICE RESEARCH AND STATISTICS DIRECTORATE
ROOM 278, 50 QUEEN ANNE'S GATE
LONDON SW1H 9AT
TELEPHONE: 0171-273 2084 (ANSWERING MACHINE)

ISSN 0072 6435
ISBN 1 85893 5768